What in the World are Fairies?

Elspeth Graham

OXFORD
UNIVERSITY PRESS

OXFORD
UNIVERSITY PRESS

is a department of the University of Oxford.
It furthers the University's objective of excellence in research, scholarship,
and education by publishing worldwide in

Oxford   New York

Auckland   Cape Town   Dar es Salaam   Hong Kong   Karachi
Kuala Lumpur   Madrid   Melbourne   Mexico City   Nairobi
New Delhi   Shanghai   Taipei   Toronto

With offices in

Argentina   Austria   Brazil   Chile   Czech Republic   France   Greece
Guatemala   Hungary   Italy   Japan   Poland   Portugal   Singapore
South Korea   Switzerland   Thailand   Turkey   Ukraine   Vietnam

Oxford is a registered trade mark of Oxford University Press
in the UK and in certain other countries

British Library Cataloguing in Publication Data

Data available

ISBN: 978-0-19-846135-7

9 10 8

Printed in China by Imago

Paper used in the production of this book is a natural,
recyclable product made from wood grown in sustainable forests.
The manufacturing process conforms to the environmental
regulations of the country of origin.

Acknowledgements

The publisher would like to thank the following for permission to reproduce photographs: **p4** Chris Beetles/London, UK/Bridgeman Art Library, **p5**t Alamy/Interfoto, **p5**l The Maas Gallery, London, UK/Bridgeman Art Library, **p6**l Mary Evans Picture Library, **p6**t Corbis/Fine Art Photographic Library, **p7** Corbis/Werner Forman, **p8**t Corbis/Alexander Demianchuk/Reuters, **p8**b Alamy/JTB Photo, **p9** Art Archive, **p9**b Mary Evans Picture Library, **p10** Art Directors/Joan Wakelin, **p11**l Christies Images/Bridgeman Art Library, **p11**r Alamy/David Noble Photography, **p12** Ryogi Otsuka, **p13**t Archives Charmet/Bridgeman Art Library, **p13**c Russell-Cotes Art Gallery & Museum, Bournemouth/Bridgeman Art Library, **p14** Science Photo Library/George Roos, Peter Arnold Inc., **p15** Andrzej Gorzkowski, **p16**l Alamy/John Robertson, **p16**r Alamy/Agripicture Images, **p17**t Alamy/David Crausby, **p17**b Alamy, **p18** James Clare Photography/Photographers Direct, **p19** Corbis/Wilfred Krecichwost, **p20**t Topfoto, **p20**b Science & Society Picture Library, **p21** Science & Society Picture Library, **p22** Corbis/Reuters, **p23** Getty Images

Cover: Pat Moffett

Illustrations by Pat Moffett: **p11**, **p13**, **p15**, Mark Duffin: **p19**, David Mostyn: **p22**

Designed by Bigtop

Contents

What are fairies?

Fairies, or faeries, are found in myths, legends and folktales throughout the world.

A fairy is usually described as a spirit, or a magical creature. Fairies often look like humans but they have **supernatural powers**.

© Chris Beetles Ltd, London

The word 'faerie' was the name given to the land where the magical people of our fairy stories lived. Nowadays, 'fairy' is often used to describe the people from that land.

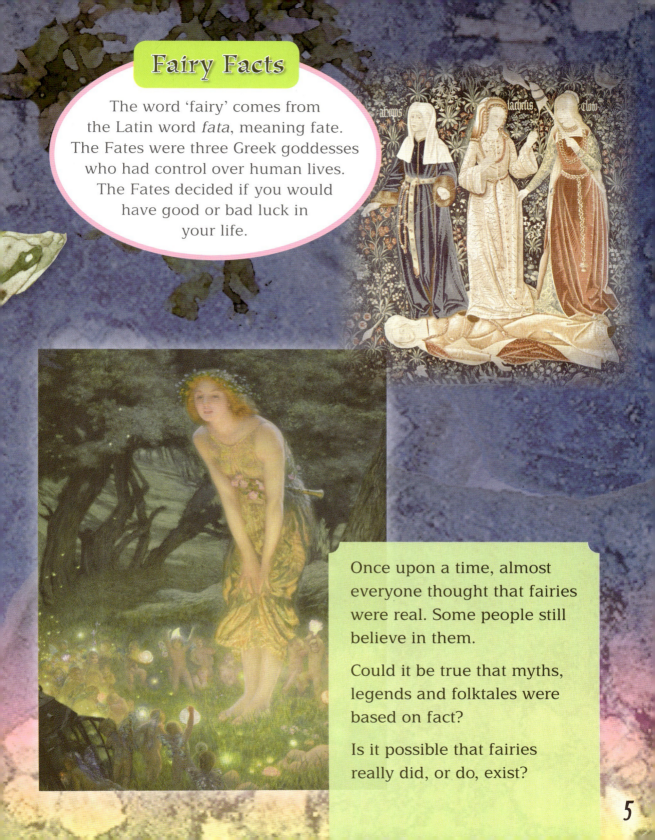

Fairy Facts

The word 'fairy' comes from the Latin word *fata*, meaning fate. The Fates were three Greek goddesses who had control over human lives. The Fates decided if you would have good or bad luck in your life.

Once upon a time, almost everyone thought that fairies were real. Some people still believe in them.

Could it be true that myths, legends and folktales were based on fact?

Is it possible that fairies really did, or do, exist?

What do they look like?

Nowadays, fairies are often thought of as tiny, young, winged females.

But at other times fairies have been described in many different ways. Sometimes tiny, sometimes tall, they can be wrinkled and hideous or beautiful and angelic. They may even be male, invisible or shape-changing spirits.

Almost every country in the world has its own fairies. Much of Europe is very rich in fairy **lore**. When people began to **migrate** to the **New World** countries they took this fairy lore with them. Some people believe the fairies went too.

Abatwa

The tiniest of fairies. They live in the **anthills** of South Africa. Abatwa are very shy and are usually only seen by children.

Bokwus

A spirit creature found in northwest America and Canada. He lives in dense forest and his war-painted face is sometimes seen peering round trees. The Bokwus takes the spirits of people who have drowned to his home.

The Bokwus

Brownies

Small, friendly, male spirits who live in people's homes. At night, they help with household tasks or with work on the farm. In return, a Brownie expects to be left a reward, like a glass of milk and some cake.

Don't offend a Brownie or he may turn into a **Boggart**.

Candelas

Tiny Italian fairies that look like twinkling lights such as these. They can be seen just as it begins to get dark.

Chin Chin Kobakama

Japanese fairies that help around the house. They always take the form of old men and women.

Djinn

Arabian shape-shifting fairies that take many different forms. They can appear as people, monsters, ostriches, dogs, cats or snakes.

Knockers

Cornish Knockers are dwarf-like fairies that live underground. Miners leave them food and drink and in return they warn the miners of danger or help them find **ore**.

Manitou

Fairies who lived alongside the Algonquin people, Native Americans from the east of America. They play tricks and make magic with their drumming. Manitou wear antlers on their heads.

Mekumwasuck

Fairy folk of the Passamaquoddy Native American peoples of northeast America. They are small and very ugly with hairy faces. If one looks directly at you, you might die or become ill.

Mimis

Long-limbed Australian fairies that live in cracks in rocks.

Mimis live in cracks because it is believed that their thin bodies would break in the wind.

Ohdows

Little people who live underground in North America. They use their magic to try to stop earthquakes.

Peris

Small, very beautiful winged
fairies from Arabia; often
friendly towards people
but can be a nuisance.
They live on **fragrance**.

Will-o'-the-Wisps

Flickering lights, seen at night over marshes and moors. If you walk
towards them they vanish and reappear elsewhere. They are also
called Jack o' Lantern, Hunky Punky, Hobbedy's Lantern and Night
Whispers.

These Will-o'-the-Wisp flickering lights may be where
the idea for the first Halloween lanterns came from.

Zips

Tiny, very shy, male fairies in Mexico. They carry spears and wear
helmets. Zips live close to deer and protect them.

Who's who in the water

Aa

Asrai

Tiny, delicate water fairies. They turn into a small puddle of water if captured.

Kk

Kappa

Japanese water creatures with webbed hands and a hollow on the top of their head. When the hollow is full of water, they are very powerful. They are also polite, so, if you meet one, bow very low. The Kappa will return your bow and the water will tip out of the hollow.

Mermaids

Beautiful female creatures with long hair and sweet voices. Usually described as human from the waist up, with the tail of a fish below. Mermaids sometimes **lure** sailors to their deaths. They are found all over the world.

Mermen

Dangerous male sea creatures. They cause storms and wreck ships.

Selkies

Seal-like creatures that live around Britain and Ireland. They can take on a human form when out of the water.

Selkies can slip off their skins to come ashore.

Why believe?

Believing in fairies was a way of explaining the unexplainable. They could be blamed for lots of things.

People thought that fairies could be spiteful and sometimes even dangerous.

The sudden deaths of animals or humans were believed to be due to 'Elf-shot'. Small flint arrow-heads (that we now know were made by Stone Age people) were thought to belong to elves.

Stone Age arrowheads or 'Elf-shot'.

Cramp, painful joints and bruises were explained away as being caused by pinches from spiteful or angry fairy fingers.

Fairy mischief was a way to blame someone else if things went wrong – if the milk turned sour or the bread didn't rise. It was no one's fault; it was the fairies.

Folklore was handed down from parents to children. Folklore told people how to protect themselves from troublesome or angry fairies.

Tangles that appeared in human hair or in horses' manes were known as 'Elf-locks'.

Keeping out of mischief

The greatest protection from fairy mischief was iron. People carried iron nails or knives in their pockets. Iron horseshoes were hung on doors to keep fairies out.

It was thought that bells kept fairies away. Bells were tied around the necks of cattle and sheep to keep them safe.

Morris Men wear lots of bells to scare off fairy spirits.

Cross-shapes on cakes and breads were thought to stop fairies from dancing on them. Dances might bewitch cakes and stop bread from rising.

Red threads and ribbons were believed to give protection. They were often tied to front doors, to the tails of cattle and sheep, and even around children.

Travellers on lonely roads would sometimes turn their clothes inside out and put their shoes on the wrong feet to make sure fairies didn't lead them astray.

Daisies and daisy chains kept fairies away.

Do people still believe in fairies?

"Fairies stop developers' bulldozers in their tracks"

The Times **21 November 2005**

Villagers in St Fillans in Scotland protested that a new housing estate would 'harm the fairies'. It was believed that fairies lived beneath a large rock in the middle of the site. The development was stopped.

Iceland is a **remote** country that has been shaped by volcanoes and ice.

Iceland is a land of fire and ice.

In a recent **poll** in Iceland over half the **population** believed that they share their land with fairy folk.

When new roads and buildings are planned in Iceland, experts in fairy **lore** are often hired to make sure that the elves and fairies are not disturbed. Engineers re-route roads around hills and boulders to avoid fairy anger.

All over the world there are people who believe in fairies. As recently as in 1998, some divers claimed to have seen a mermaid in the seas around the islands of Hawaii.

Photographs – real or fake?

The case of the Cottingley Fairies

In 1917, in the village of Cottingley, 16-year-old Elsie Wright and her 10-year-old cousin Frances Griffiths took the most famous fairy pictures in the world. Many people took them very seriously, for many years.

Arthur Conan-Doyle, the author of the Sherlock Holmes detective stories, believed these photos were **real evidence** of fairies and published them.

When Elsie and Frances were old ladies they admitted that four of the photographs were **fake**. They had cut out pictures of fairies and held them in place with hatpins.

Frances always insisted that this photograph was genuine.

There have been several **hoaxes**.

Many people, over hundreds of years, have reported sightings of fairies. But there are no genuine photographs, or other real evidence as proof.

Some people think that long ago there was a smaller race of people that lived alongside our **ancestors**. Perhaps the **universal** stories of little folk are based on these people. Is it possible that memories of such little people became our myths and legends?

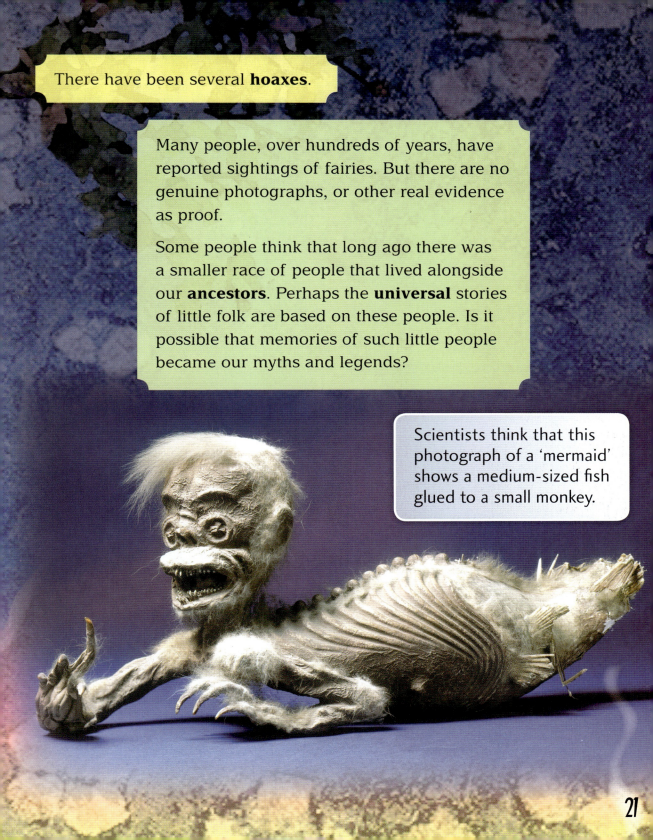

Scientists think that this photograph of a 'mermaid' shows a medium-sized fish glued to a small monkey.

Real evidence of 'little people'

On an **isolated** island, far, far away, there once lived a race of tiny people who battled with dragons and hunted miniature elephants. This may sound like a fairy story but in 2003 **archaeologists** discovered the bones of a **species** of tiny humans on the **remote** Indonesian island of Flores.

The bones show us that the tiny humans might have looked like this.

The bones of miniature elephants (stegadons) and of Komodo dragons were also found in the same cave.

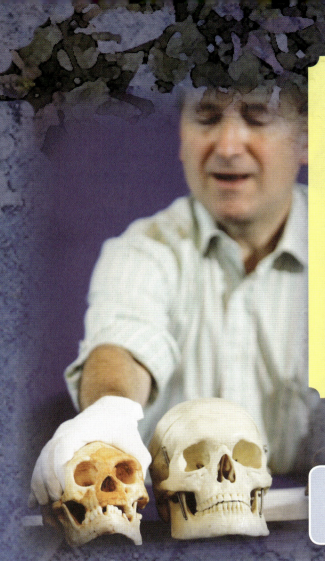

Scientists think that these hobbit-sized people lived on the island about 12,000 years ago. This means that they might have shared the island with humans like us.

Our species of human is called *Homo sapiens*, meaning the wise human. The smaller species is called *Homo floresiensis*, meaning the human from Flores. *Homo floresiensis* was about 1 metre tall.

A *Homo floresiensis* skull (left) alongside a *Homo sapiens* skull.

The Flores islanders have **legends** about little people called Ebu Gogo. The Ebu Gogo were about 1 metre high, very hairy and lived in caves. They were mischievous and even dangerous.

Were the Ebu Gogo legends that were passed down through **generations** based on fact?

Some people think that this is real evidence that the 'little people' of fairy stories did exist.

Glossary

ancestors – members of the same family who lived in the past

anthills – ants' nests that look like mounds of earth

archaeologists – people who study the past by looking at what has been left behind

Boggart – bad-tempered ugly brownies that love making a mess and breaking things

fake – false or misleading

folklore – the beliefs and stories of a group of people

fragrance – the scent of a perfume

generations – lifetimes (a mother is in one generation; a grandmother is in another generation)

hoaxes – tricks or deceptions

isolated – alone, far from other things or other people

lore – traditions or beliefs

lure – tempt a person or animal into a trap

migrate – to leave one place and settle in another

Morris Men – people who dance the traditional English Morris dances

New World – the countries that Europeans discovered, explored and settled in, such as America, Australia and New Zealand

ore – rock with metal in it

poll – a set of questions to find out what people think

population – all the people who live in a place

real evidence – an object or thing used as proof

remote – distant, a long way away

shape-shifting – a change in the form or shape of a creature

species – a group of similar animals

supernatural powers – magical powers, such as the ability to fly, to cast spells, or to see into the future

universal – found worldwide